SO-BNI-882

THE BOBBS-MERRILL STUDIES IN SOCIOLOGY

A Tottering Transcendence: Civil vs. Cultic Aspects of the Sacred

N. J. Demerath III

THE BOBBS-MERRILL COMPANY, INC.
INDIANAPOLIS · NEW YORK

MIDDLEBURY COLLEGE LIBRARY

BL
60
D454

11/1975
Soc.

Copyright © 1974 by The Bobbs-Merrill Company, Inc.
Printed in the United States of America
First Printing

Library of Congress Cataloging in Publication Data
Demerath, N.J., III.
A tottering transcendence: civil vs. cultic aspects of the sacred.
(The Bobbs-Merrill studies in sociology)
   Bibliography: p.
   1.   Religion and sociology.   I.   Title.
BL60.D454   301.5'8   73–10476
ISBN 0-672-61175-9 (pbk.)

Introduction

One of the occupational hazards of the sociologist of religion is responding to the casual query of a new acquaintance, ". . . and what do you do?" To give a forthright answer is to risk one of three reactions. The first is a gush of gratitude for having finally found a sociologist who is promoting the faith. The second is a kind of demonic delight in having discovered a new ally in the attack against religion. The third involves a quick departure in search of more stimulating company on the assumption that any sociologist interested in religion must be either sadly archaic or woefully confused.

There are no doubt a few sociologists of religion to whom each of these reactions would be appropriate. But all three are based on premises that are faulty in the main. Consider the first response and its assumption that the sociologist of religion is a proselytizer in intellectual clothing. Here it is useful to distinguish between the "sociologist of religion" and the "religious sociologist." Although both have made major contributions to the research literature, there is a difference. The religious sociologist is one for whom advancing the faith may indeed take precedence, while the sociologist of religion has a primary allegiance to scholarship. In his foremost role as sociologist, he views religion as a subject for detached analysis rather than personal commitment. His interest is theoretical rather than theological, empirical rather than metaphysical, and clinical rather than polemical. His lectures should never be confused with sermons. Indeed, in teaching courses in the subject, he is apt to take pride in such incidents as the remark of a priest who, while enrolled as a student, said he swore an oath of silence as part of his Lenten observance.

Much of this applies equally in rebutting the second reaction. Attacking a faith is no more compatible with scholarship than evangelizing for one. While the sociology of religion may have had some indirect negative influence by demystifying the forms and functions of religion and hence reducing its credibility, this has been largely incidental rather than intentional. In fact, it is ironic that some of the most significant attempts to demonstrate the sociological importance of religion were the work of persons who were themselves religiously indifferent or uncommitted—scholars such as Émile Durkheim and Max Weber, whom we shall encounter shortly. And yet, it is understandable that some might view the sociologist of religion as hostile. Like the physician, the sociologist tends to learn more by studying illness than health. He frequently seeks out instances of tension, conflict, and change as central clues in his investigation. Moreover, the sociologist often finds it useful to analyze an institution not solely in its own terms but in comparison with other institutions and with alternative models of reality. It may gall many religionists to see the church compared with the military or an asylum, but such comparisons can be instructive. In sum, the sociology of religion is areligious in its orientation, though it can be both religious and irreligious in its consequences.

But what of the third reaction, which consigns the sociologist of religion to intellectual oblivion? Of course, every scholar must answer for his own madness. But an interest in religion is neither as trivial nor as anachronistic as the charge suggests. Insofar as conventional religion is in decline, the process itself is worthy of attention. And yet, decline must not be confused with demise. Religion is still with us in conventional as well as unconventional forms. Indeed, one can define religion in such a way as to find it at the core of the most blatantly nonreligious institutions and events. Every society depends upon beliefs, rituals, shared values, and social integration of some sort. Since each of these matters has been examined closely by students of religion, it is small wonder that theories concerning the role of religion in society have provided some of the most penetrating insights into the nature of society itself.

In what follows, I attempt to provide an introductory overview to some of the concepts and insights that have made the study of religion exciting for me. As the title indicates, I think formal religion in the West is indeed tottering in its perceived transcendence over the affairs of man. But this is part of a very long-term historical process which is too important to be left to historians alone. This essay is a secular introduction in that it seeks to stand apart from the subject matter under scrutiny. In labelling that subject matter sociology of the "sacred" rather than the more conventional sociology of "religion," I mean to underline a point to be made throughout: namely, that the subject matter goes beyond religion and the church as they are conventionally understood.

This essay harbors no delusions of adequacy, much less grandeur. Space precludes an encyclopedic presentation of the field, but the nature of the assignment means that I must take pains to represent the views of others in addition to my own. In one sense, I have sought to weave a series of perspectives around some of the very best studies in the literature which might constitute a broad reading list for an overall course. But I have sought to communicate a meaningful paradigm rather than an annotated bibliography or a compendium of statistics. In seeking to prod discussion rather than end it, I have seized upon those topics that have been most vexing to scholars, on the assumption that they will likely prove most interesting to students. In fact, I have begun with a particularly pivotal issue by way of introducing some of the pitfalls that a sociological approach must avoid and some of the organizing ideas that frame the bulk of the essay to follow.

A Rock for the Ages:
Why Is Man Religious?

The question as to why man is religious has been a source of both trenchant speculation and frequent misunderstanding for as long as man has sought to know himself. The issue lies at the base of both philosophy and social science, but it has never been fully settled. This is partly because each intellectual epoch has sought its own answers in its own terms. It is also because there are some traps lurking within the question itself.

Cause vs. origin One such trap involves the confusion of causes and ultimate origins, especially as this has involved the search for the "first religious man." The confusion was rampant during the nineteenth century when "evolutionism" was in vogue. According to this intellectual doctrine, western civilization represented the culmination of a unilinear sequence of development, beginning with the first man and his most primitive society. Thus, if one is to understand truly why we are as we are, one must seek out the cause among still extant primitive societies. After all, if one can locate clues as to why the very first individuals were religious, one can certainly deduce why subsequent individuals have remained so.

This approach proved a blind alley for several reasons. While societies do evolve, there is no single unilinear sequence moving from first to last, and there are enormous intervening factors that require new theories and explanations at every stage. Even if one could isolate the ultimate origins of any pattern of behavior (a quest social scientists have long since abandoned), an origin is not a cause, and any given social phenomenon may be caused by quite different factors in other societies with different cultures and degrees of complexity. Finally, the mere premise of a first religious man postulates a falsely romantic and unduly heroic conception of religion. All this may help to account for the enduring popularity of theories in this tradition. Some come from early anthropologists such as Tylor (1958) and Müller (1878), who envisioned a handful of primitive individuals trying to cope with the terrifying uncertainties of nature and developing the fanciful explanations of religion as a substitute for knowledge. Another strand in this tradition involves the early psychoanalysts, such as Freud (1960, 1964), who portrayed the "primal" individual naively struggling to resolve the potent emotional forces at war within his psyche.

Of course, such problems do exist and compel solution. But both the problems and the solutions are filtered through a preexisting social fabric. Very few individuals invent their own religion in response to their own particular concerns and hang-ups. For most persons, religion is not something to be created anew but rather a pattern of belief and activity to be learned from others. In the process not only do we learn possible solutions to widespread problems, but we are often taught the problems themselves at a very early age. As we shall see again and again, religion is a social phenomenon which cannot be reduced to purely individual terms.

Religion vs. the Church   The foregoing is related to another source of confusion, namely, the frequent failure to distinguish between religion on the one hand and the church on the other. The distinction is more than idly analytic. There is a major difference between the spiritual religious quest and the institutionalized church which may result from it. As recently described by Thomas Luckmann (1967) and dramatized by Leonard Bernstein,[1] this difference often generates considerable tension. The birth of a new religious idea or movement is as rare as it is emotional and profound. But once the idea begins to attract followers and the movement develops some of the more permanent organizational trappings of a church, much of the original emotion and profundity is sacrificed in the interests of a stable routine and of a doctrine that can be transmitted efficiently in standardized form. From the standpoint of the original innovators, this process may seem a betrayal. But from the standpoint of the church and its quite different adherents, the process is a condition of institutional survival.

Since most theories concerning man's religion (including those of Tylor, Müller, and Freud, above) have been preoccupied with the initial religious quest, they are often unappropriate as explanations of later and more conventional church participation. After all, the behavior of the religious visionary (or "virtuoso") involves quite different factors than that of the sometime church attender who has only a vague understanding of a religious doctrine that he finds less than totally compelling. Since there are far more conventional church attenders than there are visionaries, theories that dwell on religion as a creative response to personalized fears and anxieties can only apply to the few rather than the many. Once again, we see that religion must be analyzed as a social rather than purely individual phenomenon.

Cultic vs. civil religion   As a final trap in the question, "Why is man religious?" note the implicit assumption that all persons *are* religious. Of course, as hinted earlier, one can easily define religion in such a way as to justify the assumption. It can be defined so broadly that it encompasses any and all beliefs, values, and rituals that produce social integration and give meaning to life—none of which requires reference to the supernatural, to a church, or to any other conventional "religious" aspect. From this perspective, even the most ardent atheist has a sacred bent which qualifies him as religious, and some would say that this is fortunate, for it allows a number of the newer theologians to go unmasked. Show me an individual who is totally bereft of beliefs and values, who engages in no rituals, who is completely antisocial, and who has totally abandoned any sense of meaning, and I'll show you a puppet masquerading as a person. On this basis, we might conclude that everyone is indeed religious and settle the issue once and for all.

1. To my knowledge, no composer of a mass has ever consulted a sociologist first, but Leonard Bernstein's recent "Mass" suggests what might possibly result.

And yet, there is something unsatisfying about this conclusion, resting as it does on a feat of semantic legerdemain. Important as these broad insights are, they say remarkably little by attempting to say too much, and they have a tendency to complicate analysis in an effort to foreclose it simply. For if this is religion, then what is that colloquial institution that claims the mantel while involving far smaller proportions of the population? If this is religion, then why bother with more detailed investigation of its various forms and apparitions unless one is interested in diverse exotica for their own sake? If this is religion, then what excites those troubled persons of every age who bemoan the collapse of faith and warn us of the shoals which lie ahead on the irreligious course? Surely there is something else which also deserves the name "religion." How can we avoid the confusion?

My own preference is to continue with a very broad definition of religion as a statement of the basic needs of every society and every individual, but then to distinguish among forms of fulfillment. Every society, like every individual, requires consensual values and beliefs, some element of common ritual, an enduring basis of social integration, and an orientation which contrives meaning out of uncertainty. But let us consider two different sources in the form of *civil* vs. *cultic* religion.

By "civil religion" is meant those beliefs, values, mechanisms of integration, and sources of meaning that are common and even sacred to the society as a whole but that often take the most secular guise. As described in a classic statement by Robert Bellah (1964, 1967; See also Cutler, 1968), the civil religion tends to be pervasive, and in our own society it can be readily detected in the realms of politics, economics, and education. To give two examples, the observance of a July 4th holiday may be the civil equivalent of church attendance, and the "biblical" works of Jefferson, Franklin, and others have provided generations with common beliefs and values. Of course "Americanism" as our own civil religion owes a great deal to the Judaic-Christian tradition, as Bellah points out. However, derivation from a formally religious culture is not necessary to the concept, for a "civil religion" may be completely secular in its sources.

By "cultic religion," on the other hand, I mean those beliefs, values, rituals, mechanisms of integration, and sources of meaning that are set apart as somehow distinctively sacred and that compel worship on their own terms and on the part of a group self-consciously defined in these terms. Here is the domain of conventional religion and religiosity, the realm of both the established churches and the marginal sects.

Clearly it is the cultic religion that is implied in the traditional question of why man is religious. The question is not why men hold values, but why they sometimes root their values in a conception of the supernatural; not why men engage in ritual but why they often participate in ritualized worship of nonworldly deities; not why men pursue integration but why they frequently set aside churches to provide the physical setting; not why they require a sense of meaning and purpose, but why many find orientation in a doctrine based on a leap of faith rather than rational deduction.

The point is not, however, that we should abandon civil religion in order to focus exclusively on the cultic. Quite the contrary, we can only understand the cultic against the backdrop of the civil. In fact, their relationship is so important but at the same time so problematic that it provides a major fulcrum for discussing the differences between two of the most influential figures in the development of the sociology of religion and the development of sociology itself. Let us consider them separately before bringing their insights to bear on the contemporary religious scene in the United States.

Émile Durkheim and the Civil-Cultic Amalgam

Although the son of a French rabbi who in youth once experimented with Catholic mysticism, Émile Durkheim was not a religious man except in his civil allegiance to France itself. Indeed, some have suggested that his insight concerning religion arose in large measure because he only turned to the subject for theoretical rather than theological reasons.

Durkheim lived from 1858 to 1917. The kind of mediocre student who provides hope for late-blossoming intellectuals everywhere, Durkheim's scholarly career took off quickly after the completion of his first major work (and dissertation), *The Division of Labor in Society* (1893, 1947). This work and his next study, *Suicide* (1897, 1951), established his career concern with the sources of societal cohesion and the problems of social disorganization. And yet, these early works were not completely successful. In both, Durkheim sought to explain societal integration largely in terms of the structural relationships that tied men to each other through bonds of mutual interdependence. As Durkheim grew dissatisfied with this approach and became more concerned with the *moral* basis of solidarity, his interest turned to religion. In keeping with the evolutionism of his day, he sought first to understand the relation between religion and society at their simplest level among the so-called primitive tribes. Specifically, he took armchair advantage of field reports concerning a primitive Australian tribe, the Arunta. The resulting book, *Elementary Forms of the Religious Life* (1912), remains a living classic rather than an ancient relic.[2]

Durkheim's writing style is somewhat like that of the mystery writer who wants his readers to endure a bit of creative suspense before finding out the culprit. Here the mystery concerns the sustaining sources (rather than original causes) of primitive religion. Durkheim begins by reviewing some of the popular anthropological theories of the day, all of which assumed that

---

2. Readers interested in exploring the literature on primitive religion further should be aware of a number of subsequent works, including Malinowski (1955), Goode (1951), and Swanson (1960). While most of the studies are by anthropologists such as Malinowski, both Goode and Swanson bring the perspectives and techniques of sociology to bear on the topic.

the answer lies with the peculiar nature of the primitive mind. After finding these arguments wanting, Durkheim begins to construct his own.

He takes as his central clue the tendency of tribe members to make a basic ritualistic distinction between the *sacred* and the *profane*. This relates to the particular religion of the Arunta, a form of "totemism," in which some things (an animal, a tree, a bird, perhaps) are set apart and given both special protection and special veneration while other seemingly comparable objects are given no such status or recognition. Since there is nothing intrinsically more sacred about those things that are set apart as opposed to those that are not, Durkheim speculates that the quality of sacredness is imputed. That is, the "sacred" objects are merely symbolic representations of something other than themselves that is sacred in its own right. But what is it? The answer is nothing less than the society itself. In Durkheim's own words, religion is . . . "before all . . . a system of ideas with which the individuals represent to themselves the society of which they are members, and the obscure but intimate relations which they have with it" (1912, p. 257).

Note, then, that at least for the Australian preliterates in Durkheim's analysis, cultic and civil religion are not only interdependent but almost indistinguishable. It is virtually inconceivable that a person could be involved in one and not the other. The amalgam between the two is both symbiotic and stable. Religion gains its meaning from those aspects of civil society that compel the individual's awe and respect. Society could not exist without the reinforcement it obtains from cultic worship. To paraphrase another distinguished sociological theorist, Talcott Parsons (1949),[3] the importance of Durkheim's formulation lies not merely in the statement that religion is a social phenomenon but that society is a religious phenomenon. That is, society itself is a confection of beliefs, values, and rituals which render it a sacred entity in its own right.

Of course, it is ludicrous to attempt to summarize such an important theory so briefly. On the other hand, it is at least arguable that one test of a theory's greatness is the extent to which it is amenable to concise restatement. But if Durkheim measures up on this count and many others, there are a few on which he falls short. In fact, some allege that he is more provocative for the magnificence of his errors than the accuracy of his insights. In large part, his errors are those of overstatement rather than simple stupidity. Thus, in his zeal to make his point, he sometimes made it too well and too tightly, with resulting problems of circularity and tautology. In his effort to communicate convincingly, he often fell into the trap of "reification" whereby an abstraction, such as society, is described as if it were an animate being with a consciousness and purpose of its own. Certainly many critics have chided Durkheim for oversimplifying the nature of so-called "simple" societies. There is no question that his depiction makes all too little provision for the kind of conflict and change that confront all societies at some point, even the most blissfully primitive among them.

3. *The Structure of Social Action* is an interpretive classic which lays much of the groundwork for the concept of "civil religion" as well as for developments in sociological theory at large over the past thirty years. See also Parsons' treatment of Weber in this volume.

In Durkheim's defense, however, it must be said that his primary objective was realized. He advanced a strikingly new conceptual perspective, one which continues to be influential at two different levels. The first involves the very general, but no less crucial, insight that religion derives a great deal of its impetus, its structure, and its function from its relationship to the wider social context. The second involves the more controversial attempt to specify the nature of that relationship. It is true that the Arunta are not alone in suggesting a fusion of the cultic and the civil elements. This description applies to many other "simple" societies too, since, after all, part of what we mean by "simple" is precisely the absence of well-developed distinctions among such various realms of society as politics, kinship, law, education, the economy—and religion. Moreover, there are even a few complex societies which are simple on this particular issue. Pre-twentieth-century Japan represents a similar merger of the civil and the cultic insofar as the emperor was at the apex of both the state and the Shinto authority structure, and it was virtually impossible to bear allegiance to one without the other (Bellah, 1957, Benedict, 1946). Even within the West, the "separation of church and state" is a relatively recent aberration against the historical backdrop of such widespread dicta as "the divine right of Kings" and the "throne of Christendom."

And yet there is no question that Durkheim was guilty of posing a somewhat exaggerated exception as a rule. The dovetailing of the civil and the cultic elements is never perfect under the most optional circumstances. Even if one allows Durkheim to retreat to the less cantankerous proposition that religion operates to "reinforce" society, questions remain. A reinforcement relationship may be true of many circumstances, but it is assuredly not the case with all of them. For a different kind of perspective, which points up a variety of other possible relationships between the cultic and the civil, let us consider the legacy of Max Weber.

Max Weber and the Civil vs. Cultic

In some respects, Weber and Durkheim bear a striking resemblance. Since Weber was born in 1864 and died in 1920, the two were contemporary giants involved in taking some of the first giant steps on behalf of sociology as a whole. Weber was certainly as involved with the civil destiny of Germany as Durkheim was with that of France. In addition, Weber's interest in cultic religion was also the result of scholarly pursuits rather than any personal commitment.

But there were striking differences, too. Durkheim had emerged from the dual traditions of evolutionism and positivism, both of which sought rigid and overarching theoretical answers to fundamental questions, and both of which encouraged analysis of larger societies as holistic entities in their own right. By contrast, Weber was heir to quite different intellectual currents (Bendix, 1960). He shared the historian's preference for the particular over the general; he preferred to abstract certain aspects of reality and distill their pure essence in the form of "ideal types" rather than construct any grand theoretical scheme. Indeed, he was suspicious of all such schemes including one in particular, that of vulgar Marxism. While he appreciated many of Karl Marx's basic insights and never rebutted the tradition fully, Weber's work has often been described as essentially a reaction to the Marxian enthusiasm. For one thing, Weber reemphasized the importance of cultural as opposed to economic and material factors in the process of history. For another, he gave distinctive emphasis to the role of organizational forms and structures in the dynamics of social change rather than focusing on social class phenomena exclusively.

In all of this, Weber was a renaissance man of the social sciences as opposed to Durkheim who was a sociologist to the core. Weber was trained in law, history, and economics; he wrote in impressive depth on subjects as diverse as music, architecture, ancient history, and comparative cultures. But Weber was no dilettante. Each of these topics was treated from the standpoint of several common themes which also differed from the Durkheimian motif. If Durkheim was concerned with the universal sources of order and cohesion, Weber was fascinated by the particular sources that characterized the Western world. In particular, he was fascinated by the peculiar phenomenon of Western *rationality* and the degree to which Western culture had come to revolve about it. In his various efforts to explain this development, he manifests both awe and repulsion in the face of it.

With this brief introduction, let us turn to Weber's work on religion. Actually, some of Weber's analyses deal with situations that verge on the Durkheimian in that they involve relatively close convergences between the civil and the cultic. This is true, for example, of his work on Confucianism and *The Religion of Ancient China;* on Hinduism and *The Religion of Ancient India;* and on *Ancient Judaism.* In each of these cases, Weber was aware that the religion had reinforced the traditional society and its cultural patterns. But Weber was aware that other relationships between religion and society were also possible. In particular, he was sensitive to some of the contrasting relationships manifested by developments in Western society since the advent of Christianity.

It is here that Weber's distinctive perspective and conceptual contributions come into sharper focus. Throughout Weber's analysis of Western religion, one gets the impression that religion is somehow set apart from society, that its importance lies in offering both a challenge and an alternative to the social mainstream while goading social change and social transformation. Whereas Durkheim's work on "simple" societies led to a view of religion as a reinforcement for society itself, Weber's work on complex and differentiated societies gives special emphasis to another role for religion: namely, that of *reform.* In Weber's view, this is not only among the most interesting but also among the most noble functions. Indeed, if Durkheim regarded the civil-cultic reinforcement as religion at its zenith, Weber

11

tended to view this as religion as its nadir, a point reached only after a partic-ular religion had lost much of its initial thrust and had been forced by organizational and societal pressures to compromise its original principles and visions. In all of this, we see an illustration of a point made earlier. Durkheim tended to emphasize whole religious traditions, while Weber was far more concerned with specific religious movements and their distinctive processes and impact.

But Weber was more than a mere chronicler of such movements. He sought to understand them within a grid of "ideal-typical" distinctions de-signed to elucidate some common patterns. Consider three such distinc-tions as examples.[4] First, Weber was aware that religious movements do not just spring up naturally like social mushrooms after a cultural rain. Most movements develop around a particular prophet who is reacting against the social and religious traditions of the day. However, the kind of prophet and prophecy make a difference. Weber distinguished two types of special significance: the *emissary* prophet who counsels his followers to leave the society and journey inwards in the search for self-purification, and the *exemplary* prophet who seeks to lead his followers against the society in an effort to change it. If the former type of prophecy is more common in Eastern religion, the latter is more prevalent in the West. Both types, however, involve yet another ideal type in Weber's terms; that of "charismatic" authority.

In distinguishing between "charismatic," "traditional," and "rational-legal" authority, Weber was more concerned with the attitude of the follower than the characteristics of the leader. Indeed, the three are formally presented as types of "legitimations" of authority. In the *charismatic* in-stance, the follower is spellbound by the special and seemingly magical properties of the leader himself—though these properties may be imputed to the leader by the followers. In the *traditional* case, the leader is followed because leaders in such situations have always been followed and to do otherwise would be to disavow the past and upset the present. Finally, the *rational-legal* type involves authority which is exerted according to a formal set of rules and codifications agreed to by all concerned. (Here is the root of "bureaucracy"—yet another Weberian ideal-type.) In Weber's view, most religious movements begin with charismatic authority. Many religions re-main there and end there; others move on to the traditional stage (for example, the Catholic case of the papacy); only a few achieve the rational-legal level, and if they do, the movement may have purchased stability at the price of its initial spirit or inspiration. Although Weber disavowed any *necessary* succession among the three types in the development of organi-zations, religious or otherwise, the three do provide an implicit theory of organizational development which has intrigued many subsequent scholars.

Finally, as a third ideal-typical distinction, consider the difference be-

4. Weber's religious ideal-types are best developed in his later work, *The Sociology of Religion* (1963). This volume is excerpted from the extensive analytic tour de force which was interrupted by Weber's untimely death. It is a far more sophisticated and systematic work than the earlier essay on *The Protestant Ethic and the Spirit of Capitalism* (1928). It also covers a much broader range of religious phenomena.

tween "sect" and "church." This is certainly the most widely used and enduring of the distinctions we have considered thus far, but fairness compels the acknowledgment that Weber himself borrowed it from others.[5] The distinction between sect and church is in some respects a catch-all for many other differences, which Weber and others suggested, between the initial religious movement and the full-fledged religious monolith. Like many of Weber's distinctions, it has a number of dimensions to it. Thus, the *sect's* relation to the surrounding society tends to be characterized by considerable disaffection and even hostility, whereas the *church* has made peaceful reconciliation with its societal context. Sects tend to recruit their members from among the lower classes and pariahs of society, while churches appeal to those who are comfortable in society, and hence develop a higher status clientele. The sect tends to emphasize other-worldly and more bizarre theological elements, while the church tends to be more intellectually and secularly accommodating. Sects emphasize the importance of spontaneous worship and emotional participation of its members, but churches emphasize a more formalized ritual with far greater emphasis on routine. The sect emphasizes lay leadership of the spiritually elect; the church stresses professional leadership by a trained clergy. Finally, sects have relatively rigorous standards for the conversion of the few, but the church tends to embrace the membership and participation of the many on a relatively nondiscriminating basis. In all of this, one sees again an implicit organizational theory. As we shall see later, many scholars since Weber have elucidated a seemingly natural dynamic whereby sects tend to develop into churches over time, especially after the first flush of enthusiasm begins to wane and the hard abrasions of organizational reality begin to scratch. Later we shall see evidence that the opposite process, by which churches become sects, may be increasingly pertinent in the contemporary United States.

But enough abstraction. Let us seek out an illustration. One possibility would be to consider the entire historical development of Christianity as a case in point (Demerath and Hammond, 1969, chap. 2). Thus, Jesus might be viewed as an exemplary prophet, though with some inclinations to the emissary. Development from the sect of the apostles through the renaissance monolith of Catholic traditionalism into the church's current bureaucratic and rational-legal forms might be used to exemplify the shifting legitimations of authority. Finally, who can deny the abundant illustrations of sect and church which are scattered throughout the Western religious record? Weber commented on virtually all of these phenomena, but he reserved his most pungent and provocative analysis for one particular development within this broad sweep; namely, the emergence of Protestantism.

"The Protestant ethic and the spirit of capitalism" Despite an enormous output of writing, Weber is best known for this one, relatively slender, essay (Weber, 1928). It is here that Weber advances the thesis that continues to

---

5. For a much fuller exposition of the church-sect distinction and the addition of a third type—mysticism—which we shall explore later, see the work of Weber's student and compatriot, Ernst Troeltsch (1932, esp. Vol. I., pp. 328–354).

haunt social scientists everywhere, for it is here that Weber does most obvious battle, not only with Marx, but with Durkheim, too. This is not the place for an extensive exegesis of the argument; after all the book is both brief and uncomplicated enough to be read in its own right. But the basic thesis can be summarized quickly, if carefully. Thus, the rise of a distinctively new Protestant theology from the sixteenth to the eighteenth century provided a sharp challenge to the traditional Catholic ethic which had dominated Europe. Protestantism changed considerably between and after Martin Luther and John Calvin, and it ultimately evolved from a doctrine of formal predestination to one that suggested that man could, in fact, earn his salvation in the life beyond by achieving success in this life. This carried enormous appeal for the middle-class bourgeois entrepreneurs who required a more favorable ethic for their rational capitalistic endeavors. It was on the basis of this "affinity" between the developing Protestant theology and the new economic enterprise that Protestantism grew from a series of struggling bands (Lutheran, Presbyterian, Baptist) to a group of flourishing denominations. Note that Weber did not argue that the rise of Protestantism actually *caused* the emergence of capitalism. Unlike his critics who have misinterpreted him in this regard, Weber was careful to argue only that Protestantism was a "necessary but not sufficient" condition for the full flowering of the rational-capitalist ethos. In fact, the later Weber gave even less importance to such nonmaterialistic factors on the basis of his comparative work on China, India, and ancient Judaism.

To return briefly to the three ideal-typical distinctions with which we grappled earlier, Weber's essay on Protestantism provides ample, if largely implicit, illustration of each. Like any instance of historical reality, however, Protestantism tends to fall between ideal stools. Thus, the original prophetic leadership of figures like Luther and Calvin was certainly "exemplary" in consequence, but it was partly "emissary" too. Neither Luther nor Calvin thought to rally an army in behalf of major social change, and both would have blanched at the prospect of capitalism itself. Still, while their prophecies were primarily designed to blaze a more efficacious path to individual salvation, they did encourage men to participate in the world rather than to withdraw from it. Turning to the three-fold distinction between various legitimations of authority, both Calvin and Luther were charismatic in their own way, as were other theologians who followed in their wake. And yet, Protestantism, like virtually every other enduring religious movement, began to cultivate the legitimacy of tradition as well. In fact, it did not take long for northern European Lutheranism to develop many of the traditional trappings that had so long characterized southern European Catholicism. Much the same is true of gradual refinements in the leadership and structure of denominations now referred to as Episcopalian, Presbyterian, and even Baptist. While none of these denominations was developed to the point where authority was legitimized on strict rational-legal grounds, all of them incorporated some of this aspect in their codification of leadership training and organizational procedures. Finally, it goes almost without saying that virtually every Protestant denomination has made the transition from sect to church in some fashion or another. While it is true that some were more sect-like in their origins, and some have become more church-like in their development, the basic dynamic is apparent in each case.

As important as these concepts may be, however, the real thrust of Weber's essay and the controversy surrounding it concern other issues. First, is the work an accurate reading of the history of either the development of Protestantism or the rise of capitalism? While sociologists are inclined to give Weber the benefit of the doubt, historians have not been so charitable (Samuelsson, 1964; Demerath and Hammond, 1969). Many have pointed out that there were ample evidences of capitalism prior to Protestantism, that capitalism occured in other contexts such as Japan where there was no Protestant impetus, that Protestant theology was not as sympathetic to the new entrepreneurial spirit as Weber alleged, and that closer reading of the subsequent evidence suggests that Protestants are no more capitalistic than Catholics in many crucial respects. It is true that Weber made some rebuttals to these arguments (e.g., he was discussing only one particular type of capitalism, namely, the "rational" variety so distinctive to the West; he was concerned with the "spirit" of Protestantism rather than its letter or the motives of its founders; and he was more concerned with the ultimate influence of the movement on a wider culture rather than its impact on its particular adherents.) In all of this, Weber wins a few points and loses a few. Clearly, he loses enough so that the lasting significance of his essay must depend on more than its reading of the historical facts. While these facts are important, the crucial question for our purposes is not whether Weber, the historian, was right or wrong, but rather whether Weber, the theorist, was on target or off.

Alas, here, too, the jury is split. At its very broadest level, Weber's argument is unexceptionable. Thus, the realm of culture and abstract values is indeed important to society and to social change. Moreover, in a complex and differentiated society, the cultic may indeed depart from and challenge the civil, possibly producing a major change in the process. But if all of this is "possible," the question remains, is it likely? In the view of many, Weber, like Durkheim, sought to contrive an implicit rule out of a somewhat dubious exception. Some have argued that the theoretical argument woven out of the Protestant case is too simplistic to merit more general application.

Let us try another interpretation of the events that salvages Weber's basic point concerning the importance of religion but makes the point in a different way. On the basis of the various critiques of Weber's history, it is possible to create an alternative historical panorama of change with a somewhat different theoretical message. Thus, the rise of Protestantism was indeed instrumental to the development of capitalism, but not for the reasons Weber indicates. In fact, Protestantism's significance may have had very little to do with the theological particulars with which Weber was concerned. Its more important contribution was to challenge not only Catholic domination of the Western world as a whole but the ethical domination of cultic religion of any sort. Since suddenly there was more than one religious voice worth listening to, no single religious voice could be quite as compelling as in the past. Capitalism was aided not by the rise of a new and especially sympathetic theology but rather by a reduction of the obstacle posed by all theologies to any new economic enterprise. After all, as Weber himself made clear, the "rational capitalism" of the West was more than a new economic routine. It was a new cultural spirit whose ultimate success depended on reducing the credibility of some of its cultural opponents so that it could establish a new and relatively autonomous ethic of its own.

It is in these terms that the Protestant reformation may have had the greatest impact on our own age. The reformation marked the beginning of the end of cultic domination over civil affairs. The rise of capitalism, together with a variety of other secular developments including the eighteenth-century intellectual period of the Enlightenment, involved a gradual shifting in the balance of power between the cultic and the civil. Indeed, as we now turn to the contemporary religious scene, we turn to a period in which the roles have been reversed and the civil holds rather unambiguous sway.

The Contemporary Scene:
Civil Dominance and Cultic Response

To shift from the Australian Arunta to the sixteenth-century European Reformation and then to the contemporary United States is like playing hopscotch in a Wellsian time machine. The United States of the 1970s offers a sharp challenge to any theoretical system concocted elsewhere. But precisely because our situation seems so distinctive, we need all the theoretical perspective we can muster in seeking to understand it.

It would be unfair to both Durkheim and Weber to overlook their mutual anticipation of our present situation. As noted earlier, Durkheim had no illusions that the Arunta were representative of all societies. He was well aware that religion in the West was quite different and becoming increasingly so. Indeed, he speculated at length on the emergence of a secular morality to replace a formal religion that was becoming more and more archaic and out-of-step with its times.

Weber, too, was mindful of a looming loss of significance of conventional cultic religion. While he was not sanguine about the adequacies of any alternatives, Weber knew that the twentieth-century Western society was likely to be unique in many crucial respects. Certainly he was aware that much of the early thrust of Protestantism had been eclipsed by the dominance of the secular ethos of capitalism itself:

> [In the Puritans' view] the care for external goods should only lie on the shoulders of the saint like a light cloak, which can be thrown aside at any moment. But fate decreed that the cloak should become an iron cage. . . . To-day the spirit of religious asceticism . . . has escaped from the cage.

> But victorious capitalism, since it rests on mechanical foundations, needs
> its support no longer . . . and the idea of duty in one's calling prowls
> about in our lives like the ghost of dead religious beliefs (Weber, 1928,
> pp. 181–82).

In all of this futuristic speculation, Weber and Durkheim had considerable company among intellectuals during the second half of the nineteenth and the early twentieth century. The decline of conventional religion was a prophetic motif running rampant through the works of scholars as diverse as Saint-Simon, Comte, Marx, Freud, and Troeltsch. Almost any of these scholars would have agreed with the arguments of the lesser known J. M. Guyau in his book of the time, *The Non-Religion of the Future* (1962).

In one sense, then, we are now in the unique position of being able to assess the theoretical predictions of some of the great minds in the tradition of Western social thought. After all, the United States does qualify as a kind of test case. Many of the social trends that were apparent at the turn of the century seem to have accelerated to breakneck speed. Many of these trends have had direct implications for the role of cultic religion specifically. Let us consider several examples, beginning with one which is implicit in the last section.

Differentiation, delocalization, and secularization If one sought to capture the overall contribution of the Reformation period in a single snare of sociological jargon, one might refer to the process of *"structural differentiation."* This is a process whereby a society's various structures and institutions develop new autonomy and are no longer part of a single, seamless, societal web. In the United States, this process has been greatly abetted by quantitative growth with qualitative consequences. The result is not merely that cultic religion is more removed from the civil mainstream. The very concept of a mainstream is itself debatable since virtually every major institutional sector has found water of its own, whether eddies or rapids.

In one sense, this pulling apart of the social structure means that it is even somewhat far-fetched to talk of a "society"—at least in the strict parlance of the nineteenth century. In the view of many, the United States has become a political and geographical shell hosting a congeries of discreet and relatively autonomous spheres of activity. It is true that individuals play multiple roles which range among the different spheres. But the sense of structural cohesion is frequently absent. From the standpoint of cultic religion, this means two things. First, the church is perceived as less relevant to and less involved with the affairs of other institutions; hence, it is less salient from the standpoint of its actual or potential members. Second, even where the church has considerable internal thrust and relevance, it has few outside allies and little leverage through which to realize its potential impact.

Hand in glove with the process of differentiation comes another series of changes, which might be lumped under the awkward term *"delocalization."* The reference here is to the gradual loss of meaning and the actual crumbling of various local support structures which once served to encapsulate the individual and provide him with both emotional succor and social orientation. While it is easy to overestimate the shift from an extended to a nuclear family, the breaking up of neighborhood ties and sensitivities, and the blurring of ethnic identities with the acculturation of subsequent ethnic generations, there are long-term trends which have taken their toll, especially as these are exaggerated in the minds of those involved. It is a well-known sociological dictum that even fictitious events can be real in their consequences as long as they are believed and operated on. To give a classic example, consider the phenomenon of social mobility. Recent empirical studies have indicated that the actual rates of net mobility up and down the status system have not changed very much in the last 100 years. Still, many people have acted on the assumption that mobility is not only more available to them but more expected of them. This has led to new forms of activity as well as new views of self in relation to the social context.

In all of this, implications for traditional cultic religion are once again readily apparent. One might think that cultic religion would take on increased importance in filling the void. While this is no doubt true in some circumstances, it is by no means the rule. Indeed, cultic religion has always depended upon drawing a major portion of its adherents from among those who are stable in their social patterns and who see religion as an inextricable part of a closely knit fabric of social activity. Once this fabric begins to pull apart, religion suffers in the process. At the very least, it should experience major shifts in the sources of its membership and its consequent program priorities. It is conceivable that, under such altered conditions, cultic religion may diminish as a societal phenomenon or even a group phenomenon, becoming instead far more individualized in its structure and function.

Finally, it is worth noting another major motif of change, which is related to the foregoing. The process of *"secularization"* is commonly invoked with reference to religion, but it applies to a much broader range of social and cultural phenomena as well. Basically, secularization involves a demystification of the sacred and a process through which ideas and objects previously set apart and venerated on their own terms are subjected to newly critical and comparative judgments. Obviously, an increase in secularization is related to the increase in education and the increasing emphasis on rational and scientific scrutiny in general. And yet, the nature of that relationship remains ambiguous. It is at least as plausible to argue that the process of secularization has *caused* the rise of education and rationality, as the reverse. While the truth no doubt involves a complicated interaction, it is clear that secularization owes a great deal to the structural trends of differentiation and delocalization reviewed above. Once one loses the sense of urgent relatedness to ideas and objects in one's social space, it is much easier to take a critical attitude toward them. While all of society is vulnerable to this process, including the most cherished ideals and persistent values of its civil religion, traditional cultic religion is obviously in special jeopardy. Insofar as all cultic religion revolves about a core of dogma requiring a "leap of faith" as part of the act of worship, secularization can be very threatening indeed. It is in this sense that the rumored "death of God" is such an important barometer. For perspective on this development, it is worth consulting Anthony Towne's satirical, *Excerpts From the Diaries of the Late God* (1968).

In describing the three processes of differentiation, delocalization, and secularization, I don't intend an exhaustive list of the changes which buffet us, any more than I mean to issue ultimate pronouncement on the social pathologies of our time. There are certainly other patterns of change; and it is far easier to make grandiose assertions concerning change than it is to marshall supporting quantitative evidence. While it is always somewhat tempting to play social critic and conjure up visions of a society that is so distorted and discordant as to offer solace to none and malice to all, nothing could be further from my intent here. I am convinced that the overwhelming majority of the nation's citizenry are no less happy or well-adjusted than those of other societies in other times. I am further convinced that many intellectuals of all stripes tend to project their own feelings of marginality and alienation onto those whom they are analyzing. At the same time, it is clear that our society is far from static and that it has undergone some particular changes that have had special consequences for the role of cultic religion within it.

American religion in historical perspective Assessments of American religion over the last 100 years have included more than a dollop of both hyperbole and hypocrisy. America has often been described as "the most religious nation in the West." Such descriptions generally have been based on superficial evidence and frequently have been self-serving. At the risk of raising hackles on the backs of church historians everywhere, it is more than merely plausible to argue that the crucial relationship between cultic and civil religion has been weaker for the United States during the nineteenth and twentieth centuries than for almost any other Western nation. If one examines the comments of astute foreign observers on the American scene in the nineteenth century—observers such as de Tocqueville (1964) and Martineau (1962)—one finds an almost incredulous description of the discrepancy between religious appearances and religious impact. By the late nineteenth century, Weberian capitalism and Yankee industrialization had joined potent forces with other political and cultural currents of the age to force cultic religion to the back pews of the civil church. Accounts of this period by Henry F. May (1949) and Martin Marty (1961) are only two of many with a common message.

By the beginning of the twentieth century, it was even clearer that religion was on the defensive. While bursts of cultic evangelism remained common, these were quite different from the kind of quiet influence that is characteristic of an institution actually wielding power. As Liston Pope demonstrated in his classic and graphic study of the role of the churches in the midst of an economic crisis in Gastonia, North Carolina (1965), religion had become more of a handmaiden than an iron fist by the time of the Depression in the 1930s.

By this time, however, major changes had begun to occur within cultic religion itself as the major denominations adapted to changing society and their changing role within it. In particular, they began to sense that a doctrine and an ethic that were appropriate to the early nineteenth century might no longer be appropriate under the changing conditions of the mid-twentieth century. With the advent of the Social Gospel movement in American Protestantism and the rise of social conscience in American religion generally, churches began to make their appeal on different grounds. By and large, cultic religion no longer saw itself as a major political force with veto power or the right of initiative in American society. Instead, the church began to offer both criticism and respite from its position on the margins and in the interstices. At this point, religion began to undergo the heralded religious revival of the 1940s and 1950s. While this revival is often overestimated in both statistical and religious terms, there is no question that it involved at least a slight upswing in the proportion of church membership in the society and the rate of church attendance. What is important to realize, however, is that it was not a return to the religion of yore. Indeed, the revival depended on a deemphasis of that religious strain. To put it most succinctly, the revival was not a counter to secularization within the churches: the revival depended upon it.

But if revival was the church's hopeful byword through the middle 1950s, it hardly applies today. If one looks at the current cultic scene from the standpoint of the churches, there is far more justification for pessimism than optimism. Consider some of the evidence.

The two most common barometers of the religious climate are rates of church membership and church attendance. For the first time in the nation's history, the proportion of church members in the population has begun to drop off from a high of 65 percent in the early 1960s to less than 60 percent currently. These data are notoriously poor, and the change is not yet precipitous. Still, those tending the religious store and minding the budgets are concerned, to say the least. As for the percentage of the population attending church in a typical week, it has dropped steadily from a high of 49 percent in 1955 to a low of 40 percent as of 1972. Again, the change is not statistically dramatic, and it is worth noting that the United States retains a higher rate of church attendance than most Western European nations (in Great Britain, for example, the rate is 20 percent). But this is small comfort to the clergy, many of whom predict that the downward trend will accelerate.

And yet, drops in membership and attendance rates may constitute only the tip of the iceberg which looms before the churchly ship. Religious belief is also showing signs of a rapid waning. While there are no good studies available of long-term trends in the level of belief in the general population, there are a number of studies of specific population groups which are revealing. Several studies of college students show significant shifts. According to recent research by Dean Hoge (1969) comparing the level of religious commitment and belief over the past fifty years, student orthodoxy was high in the 1920s, low in the 1930s, high again in the early 1950s, and has been on a steady descent ever since. But college students are not alone in experiencing doctrinal apostasy; it is also present in the population at large and even within the churches. Thus, clergymen themselves have evidenced a decline in doctrinal orthodoxy over the past thirty years.[6] As for church members, a recent study by Charles Glock and Rodney Stark (1968) asked national samples of church members for their reaction to the statement: "I know God really exists and I have no doubts about it." Perhaps it is not surprising that fully 78 percent of the Unitarians expressed some disagreement, but note that this was true of some 33 percent of the Presbyterians, 28 percent of the Episcopalians, 22 percent of the Methodists, 30 percent of all American Lutherans, 15 percent of Catholics, and even 10 percent of the members of the Protestant fundamentalist sects.

Finally, what does all this mean for cultic religious influence in the civil arena? There are a number of clues here which are equally negative. For example, recent research suggests that the gaps between religious groups on nonreligious matters are closing rapidly. If there was ever a major difference of opinion between Protestants and Catholics on political and economic issues, such differences are very slight, indeed, today according to replications of Gerhard Lenski's work on *The Religious Factor* (1961).[7] To the extent that American religious communities ever acted as social communities virtually impenetrable to each other, this has also given way to change. Will Herberg once talked of the three major religious communities as Protestant, Catholic, and Jewish (Herberg, 1960).[8] It is now clear that intermarriage has made substantial inroads, and according to recent evidence summarized by Samuel Mueller (1971), the new communities are white Christian, white non-Christian, and Black. If one looks at the Catholic situation in particular, there is ample indication that the impact of the church on the social behavior of its adherents has become greatly reduced. According to the research of Norman Ryder and Charles Westoff *et al.* on changing American fertility practices, the percentage of Catholic women using birth control techniques formally prohibited by the church has increased from 57 percent in 1955 to 82 percent in 1970 (Westoff and Bumpass, 1973). If the church has diminishing impact on its own members in such a crucial area, it seems reasonable to expect it to have an even more diminishing impact on society at large.

Some of the most dramatic public opinion poll data currently available directly concerns the question of religious influence. For more than 15 years the Gallup poll has been asking periodically whether religion is increasing or losing its influence in American life. In 1957, only 14 percent of the national sample of adults reported that religion was losing influence; by 1965, this had increased to 45 percent; in 1970, the figure stood at fully 75 percent (Gallup and Davies, 1971). A change of this magnitude in any area of public opinion deserves to be taken seriously. The trend holds regardless of sex, race, social status, region of the country, or religious affiliation. While it is

6. For analysis of these materials as well as a variety of others bearing on the question of religious change in America, see Demerath (1968).

7. For several recent studies which throw cold water on the Lenski thesis, see Glenn and Hyland (1967), Schuman (1971), and Featherman (1971).

8. Herberg's thesis is that these groups are increasingly similar and, in an age of declining cultic significance, it is sufficient to have some religious identification—indeed any religious identification—without implementing it fully.

particularly accentuated among the young, it is present among the aged as well.

Clearly, something is up—or rather down. To put it in sociological parlance, cultic religion appears to have been eclipsed by its civil context. It is precisely in this sense that we intend the title, "A Tottering Transcendence." In fact, the phrase is redolent of a similar remark by Peter Berger (1970, p. 95): "We are, whether we like it or not, in a situation in which transcendence has been reduced to a rumor."[9] Surely the Durkheimian and the Weberian models appear wide of the mark. As for the Durkheimian relationship of mutual solidarity between the civil and the cultic, it is unreasonable to think of religion as a force for total societal cohesion in our current situation. In Richard Fenn's recent phrase, ". . . differentiation in modern societies makes it impossible—and unnecessary—for religion to provide the basis for cultural integration" (Fenn, 1972, p. 19). As for the Weberian notion of religion as a substantial force for reform and a major challenge to the status quo, this too seems an unrealistic expectation under the circumstances.

And yet, if religion is down, it is assuredly not out. Cultic religion has responded to the current situation in a variety of ways. Moreover, there are a number of functional alternatives to cultic religion which deserve at least brief mention in any introduction to the sociology of the sacred. These topics constitute the agenda for the remainder of this essay. The next section deals with the plight of the major denominations. Following this, we will consider the situation among fundamentalist groups and religious sects. Last we will briefly consider several formally nonreligious developments such as political protest, the communal movement, and the increase in therapeutic experiences.

The Church in a Post-Religious Age: Organizations in Search of a Mission

As noted at the outset of this essay, there is an inevitable tension between the pure religious quest, on the one hand, and the institutionalized church, on the other. "This is the tragedy of religion: institutionalized it becomes corrupt, without the churches it dies" (Miller, 1958, p. 347). While it would be indefensible to argue that there is no relationship at all between the organizational church and the religious spirit today, it is certainly true that the relationship has been strained by recent circumstances. Although some people have argued that religion will persist long after the churches have

9. All of Berger's books should appear on any reading list in the area if for no other reason than their elegant and provocative titles, e.g. "The Noise of Solemn Assemblies;" "The Precarious Vision;" and "The Sacred Canopy."

disappeared, one could speculate with equal evidence that the churches, as we are coming to know them, will outlast religion as we have known it in the past. Many churches have taken steps to assure their organizational survival, but these very steps have rendered them less well-equipped to provide the kind of solace and inspiration that are at the core of their traditional mandate. The problem is not one of corruption or prostitution, but rather one of adaptation to an increasingly complex and threatening social circumstance.

Bureaucratization and the problems of goals and goallessness   As Gibson Winter points out in his recent review of the organizational changes that have characterized American religion (Winter, 1968), all of the major denominations have undergone massive changes of scale in the last fifty years.[10] Thus, membership has risen enormously owing to the simple increase in the national population as a whole. This increase in size has been accompanied by a variegation of expectations. Both of these trends in turn have required a far more developed administrative structure and a far more routinized schedule of tasks and task implementation. In short, American religion has been *bureaucratized* even as it has been differentiated, delocalized, and secularized. The romantic Norman Rockwell portrait of Americans at worship in the neighborhood church of their choice must now be placed side by side with an image of denominational headquarters as a business enterprise and a portrait of the clergyman as a harrassed professional torn between different roles and conflicting demands.

While the church is hardly the only example of such organizational developments in American society, it is perhaps particularly vulnerable to them. As Paul Harrison (1959) has pointed out in his classic analysis of the American Baptist Convention ("Northern Baptists"), the other-worldly idealism of most religious groups encourages members to avert their eyes from mundane organizational processes rather than confront them openly in order to control them purposefully. As a result, there is a tendency for changes to go undebated as a response to covert organizational exigencies rather than overt organizational goals.

And yet, the question of "goals" is troublesome in its own right. One of the things that marks the church as distinct from most organizations is precisely the fact that its manifest organizational objectives are so vague from an administrative standpoint. For example, the goal of "salvation" can mean many things to many people, and it is by definition an other-worldly matter impossible to measure in this-worldly terms. Under these conditions, it is crucial that such goals be well anchored in a system of values and beliefs that lend them support and meaning. When the values and beliefs themselves are as precarious as we have seen, the problem of goals is compounded.

10. The title of this book, *Religious Identity,* suggests a social psychological study when it is in fact a highly sophisticated analysis of changing patterns of church organization. It may be that Winter intended to suggest that basic religious identities are very much in flux as a result of these organizational changes.

For all of these reasons, many churches are now floundering in a state of "goallessness," lacking both direction and thrust. Others have reacted differently with a process that has long been characteristic of organized religion: namely, "goal-displacement." Put briefly, this involves an inversion of means and ends whereby means become ends in their own right. For example, it is one thing for a church to keep up its membership and its budget in order to further the collective pursuit of salvation, but it is quite another for matters of membership and budget to become dominant objectives in their own right, wagging the dog like the proverbial tail. This has happened with increasing frequency. To use a particularly evocative term, there has occurred a kind of "basketballization" of American religion (Page, 1952) in that many churches have sought to gain and retain their membership by proliferating activities with secular appeal such as basketball teams, psychiatric clinics, and gourmet-cooking circles. Congregations frequently compete for local and national prominence, not on the basis of their Sunday worship, but rather on the size and seductiveness of their Monday through Saturday program.

Membership heterogeneity and styles of religious involvement As the foregoing suggests and as we noted earlier among the characteristics of the ideal-typical "church," the range of individual adherents in most church settings tends to be surprisingly heterogeneous. This is true not only of national denominations as a whole but of local congregations as well. Despite the stereotypes that Episcopalians are upper class and Baptists lower class, the fact is that both have considerable class variance within them. The same is obviously true of other social distinctions such as sex, age, and even political affiliation—though not race.

The whole question of membership heterogeneity raises another set of issues: namely, who among these types is most likely to be religious? Predictably, this question has spawned a considerable research literature. One important problem is a careful definition of the term "religious." Here scholars have used various distinctions, ranging from "healthy" versus "sick" souls (James, 1958), through "intrinsic" versus "extrinsic" (Allport, 1950), to recent deployment of "locals" versus "cosmopolitans" (Roof, 1972).

But one of the most elaborate and enduring theoretical schemas comes from Charles Glock and involves no less than five *dimensions* of religiosity: first, the *ritualistic,* or the extent to which people attend church services and engage in other forms of prayer, worship, and religious activity; second, the *intellectual,* or the extent to which people are knowledgeable about matters of doctrine and the denomination; third, the *ideological,* or the degree to which people hold actual religious beliefs with saliency; fourth, the *experiential,* or the extent to which religion elicits emotional reaction in its adherents; and fifth, the *consequential,* or the degree to which religion has an impact on the everyday life of the individual (Glock and Stark, 1965, chap. 4). It goes almost without saying that different types of parishioners allocate different priorities to the five dimensions, even within the same congregation. To summarize an extensive research literature far too concisely, persons who have relatively high status and are well integrated in society tend to participate most in the ritualistic and intellectual facets of religion while deemphasizing the ideological, experiential, and consequential sides. On the other hand, those persons who are somewhat marginal to the secular world—including the lower classes, the very young and very old, those with broken families, and, it has been shown, women as well—these all tend to have the reverse profile.

The conflicted clergy Perhaps the most illuminating window through which to view the situation of the contemporary church involves the plight of the clergy. Lest the term "plight" seem loaded, it is worth noting the results of a recent national survey which asked clerics whether they had ever seriously considered leaving the religious life. The answer was "yes" for 23 percent of the Catholic priests, 32 percent of the Protestant ministers, and 43 percent of the Jewish rabbis (Gallup and Davies, 1971, pp. 1–7). Clearly there are problems within the profession. Without attempting a complete catalogue, it is worth noting several of the more salient difficulties.

One problem involves a frequent discrepancy between a clergyman's formal training in the seminary and the actual job requirements which are encountered later (Gustafson, 1963; Fichter, 1961; Carlin and Mendlovitz, 1958). Since most seminaries give preponderant emphasis to matters of theology and ethics, and accord relatively little time to pastoral counseling, community politics, or church administration, it is often a rude shock when the cleric discovers that the latter skills are most in demand. Specifically, he is apt to spend as much as 75 percent of his time on administration alone (Blizzard, 1958), and here is where his training has been least adequate. Few clergymen learn to like the administrative tasks. Most would prefer to emphasize the roles of ritual leader and learned sermonizer; hence they begrudge the time they must spend on keeping the organization afloat. Many find that this administrative priority departs, not only from their own sense of role preferences, but from the preferences expressed by their parishioners as well (Glock and Stark, 1965). Like the church itself, its chief functionary labors under a major conflict between the ideal and the real.

This conflict is manifest in somewhat different terms for many clergymen who find it difficult to serve as the official embodiment of a churchly tradition about which they themselves have questions. Consider the dilemma of the typical young product of a liberal seminary. He is frequently so sophisticated in his own theology as to be unorthodox, perhaps so unorthodox that he would qualify as an actual "atheist" as the label is used by his less sophisticated parishioners. What is he to do in facing the parishioners themselves? First, he can simply present his quarrels with orthodox doctrine in a straightforward fashion at the risk of losing the backing of the supporting members of his parish. Second, he can present his doubts in the form of a new and perhaps more convoluted theology, but at the risk of emptying his pews through turgid sermons. Finally, he can simply swallow his doubts and either pretend complete faith or avoid the topic of doctrine altogether. Although none of these options is fully satisfying, the last response is by far the most popular one as suggested by the title of Charles Merrill Smith's insightful satire *How To Become a Bishop Without Being Religious* (1965). Many clergymen greatly prefer to accord little emphasis to the realm of doctrine and ritual in order to give major importance to the realm of ethics.

And yet, the matter of ethics is frequently troublesome, too. Earlier we saw the degree to which Catholic women have departed from the church's position on birth control. Catholic priests have made their own adaptation to the situation. Many have preferred to leave the issue completely up to their parishioners without getting involved. Certainly there are vast numbers of clergymen who find that a strong position on almost any ethical issue is likely to offend as many as it attracts. After all, given the heterogeneity of membership described earlier, the question arises as to which group he will define as his principal audience in taking specific positions on controversial issues. As Jeffrey Hadden (1969) has pointed out in detail, ministers are considerably more "liberal" on most issues than most of their congregants. To what extent can they serve as leader without losing their followers and indeed their pulpit? The problem is never trivial, but it is exacerbated more in some church structures than in others. Thus, there are some "polities," such as the Catholic and the Episcopalian, in which the local clergyman is answerable primarily to those higher in the denominational structure who provide support in moments of controversy. On the other hand, there are other situations, such as in the Baptist and the Congregational in which the local laity hold primary power over the hiring and firing of their clergymen; hence the minister must make his peace with them even in the midst of disagreement. The importance of the particular kind of church polity has been recently highlighted with respect to the civil rights issue. As several studies have indicated, including those of Campbell and Pettigrew (1959), Hadden and Rymph (1966), and Wood (1970), ministers in situations of the first type are far more likely to stake out prophetic positions on civil rights issues than are ministers from the second. And yet, ministers of both types find their degrees of freedom greatly limited by the political reality that impinges upon them in the typical congregational setting. In matters of ethics, as with doctrine, their most common response is to avoid a confrontation by avoiding public and unqualified stances.

Denominational headquarters and the rise of ecumenism Even under the most favorable circumstances, the relationship between the local congregation and the denominational bureaucracy poses yet another conflict for many clergymen. Although religion has traditionally witnessed a conflict between the laity and the professionals, this is now exacerbated by the extent to which many professionals, especially those on the denominational staff, have become removed from the local lay scene. Insofar as there is conflict between the laity and the bureaucratic pros, the local clergyman tends to get caught in the middle. This is true not only with respect to matters of budget, adoption of common hymnals, Sunday school texts, and the structure of various church activities. It also applies to areas of major controversy, such as the de-Latinization of the Catholic mass and recent Protestant efforts in the direction of ecumenism. Indeed, the ecumenical phenomenon is particularly revealing of many problems experienced by the major denominations.

From the perspective of national denominational headquarters, the ecumenical spirit often makes good administrative sense. After all, there is a certain economy in scale and perhaps even a safety in numbers. At a time when every major denomination has begun to feel both an economic and a political pinch, the notion of banding with other denominations so as to pool mutual resources and present a common face has enormous appeal. In fact, this appeal has been increasingly acted upon in recent years. Not only have we witnessed the emergence of the United Church of Christ as the merger of the Congregational and the Evangelical and Reformed denominations, we have also seen the joining of the Unitarian-Universalists and of the Methodists and the Evangelical United Brethren, not to mention the much-discussed possibility of even larger mergers on a far grander scale. Apart from actual mergers, there has been a dramatic increase in the degree of inter-church cooperation at national and local levels in the form of church councils and the rise of community churches representing several different denominations in a single area.

But if all of this ecumenism makes sense from the standpoint of a management expert at the national level, it frequently appears suspicious from the standpoint of the local members of a traditional church. Indeed, it is one thing to contrive an ecumenical merger "at the top" but quite another to see it implemented fully "at the bottom." Local churches have often proved highly resistant to some of the mergers developed on high, including those mentioned above. In some cases, actual lawsuits have been filed, and in other cases, ecumenical actions at the national level are effectively ignored at the local level. The problem is not one of distinctive religious beliefs so much as differences in church style and structure. Indeed, religious beliefs are among the least important obstacles to religious togetherness, while seemingly minor matters of ritual observance and church polity have loomed large. Here is another sticky wicket from the standpoint of the clergyman croquet player.

So much then for a quick summary of several dilemmas facing the major American denominations in the 1970s. The point is not that these groups are out of business or even *going* out of business. In fact, they are still big business from one standpoint even while they are experiencing considerable problems and conflicts in seeking to adapt to a changing social niche within an altered social structure. The minister is at the fulcrum of these changes, and it is no wonder that his morale is low. And yet, as a seminary student told me after one of my lectures in this vein, "I know that what you said about the church is objectively true. But I feel a little as if you told me that my wife has fat legs; the fact is I love her anyway." Certainly such love still exists despite the sociological circumstances which make it more difficult to implement and sustain.

But, if this is the situation within the religious mainstream, let us turn now to a quite different setting in the form of conservative fundamentalist religion and the religious sects. Here the statistics would seem to offer far greater hope. Here proponents of continued cultic religious vitality find their most eloquent supporting evidence.

New and Persisting Patterns of "That Old-Time Religion"

By now it should be abundantly clear that a study of American religion carries special appeal for those with a keen appreciation of the ironic. Indeed, in the grand sweep of social change, the student of religion might well conclude that after the "doxology" comes the "para-doxology." One of the most intriguing of all the paradoxes concerns the continued vigor of conservative religion against the generally acknowledged backdrop of secularization in general. Thus, if the major liberal denominations have in fact begun to lose members, the smaller conservative and fundamentalist bodies are apparently still growing and sometimes at spectacular rates. How can we absorb the finding into the perspective developed thus far?

Problems of religious statistics One approach is simply to doubt the evidence concerning the conservative trend. Surely there is justification for taking the statistics with more than a grain of ritualistic salt. As I have noted above and discussed elsewhere at length (Demerath, 1968), it is difficult to imagine a body of historical statistics more unreliable and more teeming with error than those concerning church membership trends in the United States. This is partly because the U.S. Census Bureau has eschewed the collection of even minimal religious data on the grounds of separation of church and state. Hence, the chore has been left to the churches themselves where growth claims are frequently based on more enthusiasm than evidence. There are a number of biases that enter into the yearly tallies. Thus, over the past 150 years, there has been a continuing tendency for Protestant groups to follow the lead of the Catholics in counting infants rather than adults only. Because the various Protestant denominations have made this change separately and unevenly over time rather than all at once, this has produced a continuing artificial source of inflation in the number of "members" reported overall, a trend which does not reflect any greater popularity on behalf of the church group in question. To take another example of bias which lurks in a procedure that depends upon local church bodies reporting their own tallies to national offices, there are many local groups which have not chosen to make such reports in the past and have only decided to do so fairly recently. At the time that they are included in the tally, this again produces an unnatural inflation in both the overall membership figures and the specific membership attributed to groups of their type. Since most of these recalcitrant groups are both small and conservative, this may help to account for much of the seeming upsurge in church membership of this variety. Finally, there has always been a tendency for religious groups to round their membership totals to the nearest higher number rather than the lower one, hence producing an inflationary factor which must be regarded skeptically by those seeking rigorous data. Since this tendency is also most pronounced among small bodies which lack formal accounting procedures, it tends to accentuate the apparent growth pattern of the many conservative groups that are typically very small indeed.

But despite such caveats, most scholars are convinced that there is something real as well as something fictitious in the conservative trend. While these groups are perhaps not growing as fast as their statistics would suggest, there is little question that they are growing faster than the mainstream liberal denominations which have a declining rate of growth. Again, however, one must avoid the conclusion that the small and conservative religious sects are taking the country by storm. Overall, they still account for a very small part of the population at large and even a relatively small fragment of that portion of the population that consists of church members. Roughly half of the total population can be classified as church members of some sort. Of these, fully 92 percent are accounted for by some 25 religious groups out of the more than 250 which formally exist, and only these 25 groups have as many as 500,000 members nationally. Of these bodies, there are a number which are non-Protestant, including the Roman Catholic church with some 46 million members, the Eastern Orthodox churches with another 3.5 million, and the various Jewish groups with close to 6 million. Turning to the Protestant realm where most of the fundamentalist religious action is concentrated, some 60 percent of the 70 million Protestants are accounted for by ten major denominations, and all but one of these are unambiguously "liberal" in their stance towards religion itself and the society at large. The exception involves the largest single Protestant denomination, The Southern Baptist. While this has traditionally been conservative, its actions in recent years have been much less so, particularly at the level of its denominational officialdom. If one looks only at the most fundamentalist and flamboyant sectlike groups which tend to capture the fancy of the popular observer, there are perhaps more than 200 of these bodies accounting for only 5 to 10 percent of the population at large.

And yet, it is precisely here that our interpretation is most challenged, particularly since these groups do indeed seem to be developing renewed thrust. Some religious leaders are persuaded that herein lies the answer for American religion as a whole. In his recent book, *Why the Conservative Churches are Growing* (1972), Dean Kelly argues that the mainline churches have become the victims of their own strategies in opting for deemphasized doctrine, relaxed ritual, an ecumenical embrace, and the world of social action. According to Kelly, the so-called liberal churches should take a cue from their conservative brethren and reemphasize other-worldly dogma, the requirement of high levels of commitment, and the church as a distinctive island in a secular sea. Religion should become once again a crusading, evangelizing force in man's eternal effort to both solve and perpetuate the mystery of meaning and value.

Kelly and others of his persuasion have had a responsive audience of late. Indeed, one of the most significant events on the nation's current religious agenda involves an implementation of this spirit in the form of "Key '73." This is to be a major evangelizing effort on behalf of some 150 cooperating religious groups, Catholic as well as Protestant. The goal is to take the message of Christ into every corner of the society, utilizing both the mass media and door-to-door canvasses. Some of the mainline liberal denominations so far have kept their distance from the movement while their leaders have expressed skepticism, but the movement continues to gather momentum. Indeed, it has already gathered sufficient momentum to alarm many leaders of the Jewish community who see it as a possible source of renewed anti-Semitism. The possibility is not inconceivable, especially in the light of recent studies indicating a close relationship between *Christian Beliefs and Anti-Semitism,* to use the title of the controversial book by Glock and Stark (1966).[11]

The church-sect distinction revisited To the best of my knowledge, the current planning for Key '73 involves very little consultation with sociologists of religion. However, it is a fair question to inquire what a sociologist of religion might say if asked. Many would no doubt seek perspective in the literature that has developed around the original ideal-typical distinction between "church" and "sect" introduced earlier in our discussion of Max Weber. As noted then, the distinction has cut a wide swath through the study of religion, and the work since Weber and his colleague Troeltsch has added considerable depth and dynamism to the formulation. Some of the most highly regarded research in the sociology of religion has taken up the cudgels here, including virtual classics from scholars such as Festinger, Riecken, and Schachter (1965), Richard Niebuhr (1929), Milton Yinger (1946), Benton Johnson (1963), John Lofland (1966), Bryan Wilson (1961), and most recently Gary Schwartz (1970).

As all of these works point out, the distinction between church and sect is overly simple. On the one hand, it glosses over some important additional categories of religious organization, particularly those of the "denomination" and the "institutionalized sect," which stand midway between the recalcitrant sect, on the one hand, and the fully accommodating church, on the other. Moreover, Wilson has been particularly persuasive in pointing to different varieties of sects and noting that some are more likely to move in a churchlike direction than others. Schwartz has a similar message in comparing the quite different characteristics of two traditions: those of the Seventh-Day Adventist and the Pentacostal sects. In fact, Schwartz's book

11. The methodological dispute surrounding this volume is instructive for both sociologists of religion and for students of causal inference in sociology generally. For the latest salvo in the on-going battle, see Middleton (1973).

is particularly valuable since it offers insights from an ethnographic perspective and draws heavily upon an anthropological literature that is frequently ignored by sociologists.

But what does this literature suggest for the issue before us, that is, the destiny of the conservative religious movement in the contemporary United States? One motif running throughout this literature is crucial. Whatever form the particular sect may embody and whatever theological or eschatological doctrine it may harbor, all of these groups are essentially born and sustained out of a reaction to the dominant characteristics of the society at large and the mainstream churches in particular. This *reactive* characteristic holds true, not only of sects specifically, but of conservative and fundamentalist groups in general. In fact, this may be increasingly true of all cultic religion as even the mainstream becomes "a cognitive minority" and increasingly sectlike in the altered society of the future. Thus, such groups appeal particularly to those persons who are, for whatever reasons, at odds with the prevailing social context. Of course, the sources of this marginality are many and are not restricted to low socioeconomic status. They include marginalities with respect to virtually every other form of status and role in society as well, including age, family, sex, and political ideology. They may also include short-term compounding factors such as illness or other emotional wrenches.

In all of this, however, it is important to note a crucial intervening variable as pointed out especially by the work of Festinger, Riecken, and Schachter, and by the more recent study of Lofland's. Not every person who is *objectively* dislocated or disaffected will join a conservative religious movement. Somehow the alienation must be translated into a subjective need for a distinctive haven and new experience. In addition, this must be coupled with a network of interpersonal linkages to a particular religious group, which is made to appear particularly inviting and somehow specifically set apart. The fact is that relatively few low-status persons in American society meet these additional criteria.

In sum, the growth of conservative religiosity in the United States would seem to be limited by two principal constraints. First, its appeal is likely to be restricted to those persons who are self-consciously aware of being rejected or dislocated by the dominant culture, an awareness that is not as common as the objective facts of the social structure might suggest. Second, enduring conversions to conservative religiosity require more than broadgauged evangelism or mass rallies of the "Marjoe" or Billy Graham variety (Johnson, 1971). This is not to deny that conservative religiosity will remain a potent undercurrent within American society and American religion, nor is it to deny the emergence of such new phenomena as the Jesus People and the Meher Baba cult among even middle-class youth who feel in limbo between age statuses and alienated from prevailing political ideologies.[12] Such movements will always be a part of any complex society, but they are destined by their very nature to be minority rather than majority movements.

12. See Robbins and Anthony (1972).

However, there is one further constraint on the development of cultic religion of any kind; namely, the persistence and proliferation of functional alternatives to religion. This is the burden of our next section. Insofar as it leaves the realm of formal religion altogether, it may seem to be an unjustifiable digression. But because it deals with some of the most probing and widespread attempts to grapple with the sacred in a civil religious context, it is very central indeed.

Nonreligious Structures with Religious Functions

While it would be impertinent to allege that one of the major benefits of formal religion is to provide subject matter for sociologists of religion, it is worth asking what would happen to the scholarship if all cultic religion were to disappear tomorrow. In my own perverse view, the results might even be favorable. For one thing, we could then turn to the equally intriguing topic of *irreligion.* Several sociologists have already turned in this direction, notably Colin Campbell in his recent work, *Toward the Sociology of Irreligion* (1971). As Campbell indicates, this is not as alien as one might suppose from our discussion thus far. One still has to confront questions of ultimate value and ideology, and real issues exist concerning the nature of irreligious organizations and organizational dynamics, and about the relationship between personal and organizational irreligion, on the one hand, and the dominant society and civil religion, on the other.

Here is one more source of irony, though irony in reverse of that which began our last major section on conservative religiosity. Thus, if the society and the civil religion have indeed become as secularized as we have indicated, why haven't irreligious or at least "a-religious" groups such as the Unitarians, the Ethical Culture Movement, and the American Rationalist Federation grown huge in the process? The answer is largely twofold. First, many of the mainstream churches have beat these groups to the punch in making sufficient room for nonreligious persons in their midst. Second, many other activities appeal to the nonreligious and offer more than a negative doctrine for personal sustenance. Even if every individual requires some sense of transcendence, there is no necessary relationship between the transcendent and the supernatural.

At a very broad level, it is possible to distinguish several responses open to persons who are discomfited within the dominant social context. One is to join a movement that seeks to change the society and restructure the opportunities within it; this is essentially an active response. A second alternative is passive in that it involves a withdrawal from the prevailing milieu in the company of others seeking to form a new community with new forms and values. Finally, there are other responses, which differ from the previous two in that they are more individualistic than collective and involve the assumption that the problem lies more with the individual himself rather than with the society as a whole. As we have already seen, the wide variety of cultic religion embraces all of these responses. But there are secular alternatives too. Thus, political involvement and protest constitute a secular, active expression; the communal experience offers a secular, passive framework; and the therapeutic experience can be seen as a secular avenue to individual change. Let us consider each of the three briefly, noting at the outset that all are built around some notion of the sacred.

Political activism vs. formal religiosity   Certainly one of the oldest bromides in the sociological literature on religion is the phrase from Karl Marx and Frederik Engels to the effect that, "religion is the opium of the people." Marx and Engels were suggesting, of course, that religion serves to drug the sensibilities of many persons who are objectively deprived in society. In this spirit, religion is a source of social stability since it nurtures a kind of "false consciousness" and provides a relatively harmless outlet for persons who might otherwise revolt against society itself. Clearly Marx and Engels were describing only one of many possible functions of religion, and it is possible to find innumerable instances in which religion has served to accentuate rather than dull man's sensibilities to injustice. And yet, there is certainly enough truth in the Marxian hypothesis to warrant further discussion. Specifically, there is now some supporting evidence to the effect that persons who are involved in activist political movements tend not to be so involved in cultic religious groups. Two particular studies are worth citing here. The first is Rodney Stark's analysis of British and American data (1965) which reveals that there is a negative relationship between left-wing political activity and religious involvement in general (Glock and Stark, 1965, chaps. 10 and 11). The second is the research of Gary Marx (1967) to the effect that Blacks involved in the recent civil rights movement tend not to be as involved in Black religious groups as does the Black population at large.

It is not difficult to explain either of these findings. The fact is that political movements frequently offer many of the same ingredients that make the religious group attractive. After all, who is to say that the ideology behind a given political movement is not akin to the theology characteristic of cultic religion? Certainly there are rituals in both cases, and there is ample evidence that political groups both attract and retain membership by providing a sense of integrated community. Moreover, insofar as activist politics and cultic religion offer quite different responses to society, it is easy to imagine that any individual would have difficulty straddling both. While undeniably there are instances in which religious movements have taken overtly political form and vice versa, these instances tend to be the exception rather than the rule. But the point here is not that there is a negative relationship between political and religious affiliation. After all, most people are nominally affiliated with both a church and a political party. The point is rather that, from a standpoint of those who are somehow marginal to the society, *deeper* involvement in an *activist* political movement tends to preclude and substitute for *intense* involvement in traditional religion.

Note, however, that the phrase "activist political movement" should be interpreted broadly to subsume many of the new political phenomena involved in the current "age of activism." It not only includes the various forms and factions of the Civil Rights Movement, but it embraces as well the Women's Liberation Movement, aspects of the student revolution against conventional educational patterns, the broad spectrum of activities involved with the peace movement, and a wide variety of other organized efforts concerning homosexuality, civil liberties, environmental protection, and population control. Behind each one of these causes there exists a potential functional alternative to religion in the sense described above. Insofar as the contemporary American scene has witnessed a rapid proliferation of such groups, it tends to diminish the thrust behind cultic religion in general and perhaps conservative religiosity in particular.

Old and new forms of the communal movement   In turning from the active to the passive functional alternatives to religion, the clearest current instance involves the communal movement. Of course, religion itself has spawned a steady stream of quasi-utopian communities. A number of these have proved surprisingly durable over the long run, including those of the Amish, the Hutterites, and the Mennonites. Some of the newer communes have also been born out of a cultic religious impulse, especially those associated with the so-called "Jesus freaks." But what is newest about the current communal movement is the extent to which it has taken hold among the youth in a relatively secular form. According to a recent study of the Bruderhof, a third generation commune in New York state, there are now more than 3,000 hippie communes in the United States as opposed to less than 100 which existed in 1965 (Zablocki, 1971). The study distinguishes these new "intentional" communities from the traditional communities of old. Zablocki points out that many of the former receive their impetus through drug-related experiences. In some respects, they are attempts to extend the psychedelic experience of communion and to routinize the concept of a "crash-pad."

Although I am not aware of any reliable statistics on the fate of the several thousand communes in Zablocki's estimate, he notes that the rate of failure is high and suggests that the most important difficulty is "that the collective-behavior experience and the resocialization process put individuals in touch with very intense and often long-buried primal feelings, often with disastrous results" (Zablocki, 1971, p. 325).

The fact is that communes have never fared very well in a statistical sense. Another recent sociological study reports data from the past which is less than encouraging for communal movements of the present. Rosabeth Kanter's careful analysis of some 91 experimental communities founded between 1780 and 1860 shows that only 11 were "successful" in that they lasted for at least 25 years or the equivalent of a single generation (Kanter, 1972). This in spite of one principal advantage which these communes had over the current group; namely, the tendency to involve established families and a substantial proportion of mature adults. Insofar as most of the new communes are characterized by populations of young unmarrieds, the problematics of family life pose a major strain. In addition, youth has a way of growing old quickly and changing dramatically in the process. Any movement that draws so heavily upon youth is almost inevitably precarious.

It is not difficult to see that some of the same laments that apply to the religious sect are also applicable to the secular communal movement. Both represent havens from conflict and from degradations experienced in the larger society. Both involve an effort to set up total communities on a smaller scale as substitutes for the larger community which is so dissatisfying. But the communal movement has other parallels in addition to those of the religious sect. One of these is a form of commune in its own right: namely, group therapy and the increasing popularity of encounter groups and sensitivity training.

Therapy as an "invisible religion"   Just as it is now a shibboleth that Marxism is a religion, so it has become a commonplace to note the religious aspects of the psychotherapeutic movement. Parallels are apt in both cases. After all, much of the burden of our discussion of civil religion is that any group, like any society, has its religious dimensions. But insofar as therapy —whether individual or collective—involves an intensive confrontation with the sacred and the self, it may be especially religious in quality.

A recent sociological analysis of the rise of the encounter movement and sensitivity training makes much of the religious parallel and the extent to which these therapeutic experiments may function as religious surrogates (Back, 1972). Indeed, Back likens the encounter participant to the twelfth-century pilgrim. Although there is a shift in emphasis from other-worldly to this-worldly means and objectives, a sense of mystery remains within the current therapeutic framework despite its "scientific" aura. It may be precisely this combination of the mystical and the scientific that accounts for its growing appeal. Another factor may well be the emphasis on confronting the individual member's own problems in very personal terms rather than pursuing social action or social change on a broader scale.

This emphasis on a search for privatized and personal meaning is not confined to therapeutic situations, however. Instead, the therapeutic movement may simply be an indicator of a more widespread quest, particularly among the middle- and upper-status mainstream in society. In this connection, it is worth recalling that one of the most important founders of the church-sect distinction, Ernst Troeltsch, actually posited a third form of religion, which he felt would be particularly prevalent among the middle classes in the Western society of the twentieth century (Troeltsch, 1932). This form was termed "mysticism," but the label was somewhat misleading. Troeltsch really meant a kind of religious individualism that would increasingly shy away from the institutional and sacramentalized church in favor of more personal forms of expression. According to the recent theories of

Thomas Luckmann, Troeltsch was right. As Luckmann puts it in his influential book, *The Invisible Religion:*

> *In the modern sacred cosmos self-expression and self-realization represent the most important expressions of the ruling topic of individual "autonomy." . . . the individual's natural difficulty in discovering his "inner self" explains, furthermore, the tremendous success of various scientific and quasi-scientific psychologies in supplying guidelines for his search (Luckmann, 1967, pp. 110-11).*

Luckmann sounds several fitting notes on which to end this essay, just as he provides several on which to begin it. He raises once again the distinction between religion, on the one hand, and the institutionalized church, on the other. He also underlines the possibility of a conception of the sacred that exists quite apart from cultic religion of any sort. It is in this sense that one can imagine, not only a civil religion which permeates all of society, but also a variety of private religions which inform and transcend the lives of private individuals everywhere on their own terms.

So much, then, for a brief synopsis of one scholar's view of the sociology of the sacred and the panoply of religion. This essay might well have been titled, "God Notwithstanding" to suggest its attempt to move beyond the conventional church in search of broader scholarly ground. In providing a brief introduction to an extensive literature, my main objective has been to indicate that the study of religion remains exciting however the subject matter is defined. If for no other reason, it is exciting precisely because of the debate and disagreement that lurk within the field and animate it for us all.

References

Allport, Gordon W.
1950   The Individual and His Religion. New York: Macmillan.
Back, Kurt
1972   Beyond Words. New York: Russell Sage Foundation.
Bellah, Robert N.
1957   Tokugawa Religion. New York: Free Press.
1964   "Religious evolution." American Sociological Review 29.
1967   "Civil religion in America." Daedalus 96.
Bendix, Reinhard
1960   Max Weber: An Intellectual Biography. Garden City: Doubleday.
Benedict, Ruth
1946   Chrysanthemum and the Sword. Boston: Houghton Mifflin.
Berger, Peter L.
1970   A Rumor of Angels. Garden City: Doubleday/Anchor.
Blizzard, Samuel
1958   "The Protestant parish minister's integrating role." Religious Education 53.
Campbell, Colin
1971   Toward a Sociology of Irreligion. London: Macmillan.

Campbell, Ernest Q. and Thomas F. Pettigrew
1959   Christians in Racial Crisis. Washington, D.C.: Public Affairs Press.
Carlin, Jerome and Saul Mendlovitz
1958   "The American rabbi: a religious specialist responds to a loss of authority." In The Jews, ed. Marshall Sklare. New York: Free Press.
Cutler, Donald, ed.
1968   The Religious Situation. Boston: Beacon Press.
Demerath, N.J. III
1968   "Trends and anti-trends in religious change." In Indicators of Social Change, eds. Eleanor Sheldon and Wilbert Moore. New York: Russell Sage, pp. 349–445.
Demerath, N. J. III. and Phillip E. Hammond
1969   Religion in Social Context. New York: Random House.
Durkheim, Émile
1893   The Division of Labor in Society. New York: Free Press.
1897   Suicide. New York: Free Press.
1912   The Elementary Forms of the Religious Life. New York: Free Press.
Featherman, David L.
1971   "The socioeconomic achievement of white religio-ethnic subgroups." American Sociological Review 36.
Fenn, Richard K.
1972   "Toward a new sociology of religion," Journal for the Scientific Study of Religion 11.
Festinger, Leon, Henry Riecken, and Stanley Schachter
1965   When Prophecy Fails. New York: Harper Torchbooks.
Fichter, Joseph H., S.J.
1961   Religion as an Occupation. Notre Dame: University of Notre Dame Press.
Freud, Sigmund
1960   Totem and Taboo. New York: Vintage Books.
1964   The Future of an Illusion. Garden City: Doubleday/Anchor.
Gallup, George Jr. and John O. Davies, eds.
1971   Religion in America: 1971. Princeton: Gallup International.
Glenn, Norval D. and Ruth Hyland
1967   "Religious preference and worldly success: some evidence from national surveys." American Sociological Review 32.
Glock, Charles and Rodney Stark
1965   Religion and Society in Tension. Chicago: Rand McNally.
1966   Christian Beliefs and Anti-Semitism. New York: Harper and Row.
1968   American Piety. Berkeley and Los Angeles: University of California Press.
Goode, William J.
1951   Religion Among the Primitives. New York: Free Press.
Gustafson, James M.
1963   "The clergy in the United States." Daedalus 92.
Guyau, J. M.
1962   The Non-Religion of the Future. New York: Schocken.
Hadden, Jeffrey K.
1969   The Gathering Storm in the Churches. Garden City: Doubleday.
Hadden, Jeffrey K. and Raymond C. Rymph
1966   "Social structure and civil rights involvement: a case study of Protestant ministers," Social Forces 45.
Harrison, Paul M.
1959   Authority and Power in the Free Church Tradition. Princeton: Princeton University Press.
Herberg, Will
1960   Protestant, Catholic, Jew. Garden City: Doubleday/Anchor.
Hoge, Dean R.
1969   "College students' religion: a study of trends in attitudes and behavior." Ph.D. Dissertation, Harvard University.

James, William
1958   The Varieties of Religious Experience. New York: Mentor Books.
Johnson, Benton
1963   "On church and sect." American Sociological Review 28.
Johnson, Weldon T.
1971   "The religious crusade: revival or ritual." American Journal of Sociology 76.
Kanter, Rosabeth Moss
1972   Commitment and Community: Communes and Utopias in Sociological Perspective. Cambridge: Harvard University Press.
Kelly, Dean
1972   Why the Conservative Churches Are Growing. New York: Harper and Row.
Lenski, Gerhard
1961   The Religious Factor. Garden City: Doubleday.
Lofland, John
1966   Doomsday Cult. New York: Prentice-Hall.
Luckmann, Thomas
1967   Invisible Religion. New York: Macmillan.
Malinowski, Bronislaw
1955   Magic, Science, and Religion and Other Essays. Garden City: Doubleday/Anchor.
Martineau, Harriet
1962   Society in America. Garden City: Doubleday/Anchor.
Marty, Martin E.
1961   The Infidel: Freethought and American Religion. New York: Meridian.
Marx, Gary T.
1967   Protest and Prejudice. New York: Harper Torchbooks.
May, Henry F.
1949   Protestant Churches and Industrial America. New York: Harper and Row.
Middleton, Russell
1973   "Do Christian beliefs cause anti-semitism?" American Sociological Review 38.
Miller, Robert Moats
1958   American Protestantism and Social Issues, 1919–1939. Chapel Hill: University of North Carolina Press.
Mueller, Samuel A.
1971   "The new triple melting pot: Herberg revisited." Review of Religious Research 13.
Müller, F. Max
1878   Lectures on the Origin and Growth of Religion. London: Longmans.
Niebuhr, H. Richard
1929   The Social Sources of Denominationalism. New York: Holt, Rinehart, and Winston.
Page, Charles H.
1952   "Bureaucracy and the liberal church." The Review of Religion 16.
Parsons, Talcott
1949   The Structure of Social Action. New York: Free Press.
Pope, Liston
1965   Millhands and Preachers, 2nd ed. introductory essay by N. J. Demerath III and Richard A. Peterson. New Haven: Yale University Press.
Robbins, Thomas, and Richard Anthony
1972   "Getting straight with Meher Baba: a study of mysticism, drug rehabilitation and postadolescent role conflict." Journal for the Scientific Study of Religion 11.
Roof, W. Clark
1972   "The local-cosmopolitan orientation and traditional religious commitment." Sociological Analysis 33.

Samuelsson, Kurt
1964   Religion and Economic Action: A Critique of Max Weber. New York: Harper Torchbooks.
Schuman, Howard
1971   "The religious factor in Detroit: review, replication, and reanalysis." American Sociological Review 36.
Schwartz, Gary
1970   Sect Ideologies and Social Status. Chicago: University of Chicago Press.
Smith, Charles Merrill
1965   How to Become a Bishop Without Being Religious. Garden City: Doubleday.
Swanson, Guy E.
1960   The Birth of the Gods. Ann Arbor: University of Michigan Press.
Tocqueville, Alexis de
1964   Democracy in America. New York: Vintage.
Towne, Anthony
1968   Excerpts From the Diaries of the Late God. New York: Harper and Row.
Troeltsch, Ernst
1932   The Social Teachings of the Christian Churches, 2 vols. New York: Macmillan.
Tylor, E. B.
1958   Primitive Culture, 2 vols. New York: Harper and Row.
Weber, Max
1928   The Protestant Ethic and the Spirit of Capitalism. New York: Scribner's.
1963   The Sociology of Religion. Boston: Beacon Press.
Westoff, Charles, and Larry Bumpass
1973   "The revolution in birth control practices of U.S. Roman Catholics." Science 179.
Wilson, Bryan
1961   Sects and Society. Berkeley and Los Angeles: University of California Press.
Winter, Gibson
1968   Religious Identity. New York: Macmillan.
Wood, James R.
1970   "Authority and controversial policy: the churches and civil rights." American Sociological Review 35.
Yinger, J. Milton
1946   Religion in the Struggle for Power. Durham, N. C.: Duke University Press.
Zablocki, Benjamin
1971   The Joyful Community. Baltimore: Penguin.

THE BOBBS-MERRILL REPRINT SERIES

The author recommends for supplementary reading the following related materials. Please fill out this form and mail.

Indicate number of reprints desired

___ **Barber, Bernard** 1941 "Acculturation and messianic movements." American Sociological Review, pp. 663–669. **S–332**/66710 40¢

___ **Bellah, Robert N.** 1964 "Religious evolution." American Sociological Review, pp. 358–374. **S–546**/66923 40¢

___ **Birnbaum, Norman** 1953 "Conflicting interpretations of the rise of capitalism: Marx and Weber." British Journal of Sociology, pp. 125–141. **S–26**/66435 40¢

___ **Coleman, James S.** 1956 "Social cleavage and religious conflict." Journal of Social Issues, pp. 44–56. **S–47**/66453 40¢

___ **Geertz, Clifford** 1968 "Religion as a cultural system." In Anthropological Approaches To The Study of Religion, ed. Michael Banton. Tavistock Publications Ltd., pp. 1–46. **S–696**/68714 60¢

___ **Glock, Charles Y. and Benjamin B. Ringer** 1956 "Church policy and the attitudes of ministers and parishioners on social issues." American Sociological Review, pp. 148–156. **S–399**/66777 40¢

___ **Marx, Gary T.** 1967 "Religion: opiate or inspiration of civil rights militancy among Negroes." American Sociological Review, pp. 64–72. **BC–194**/67575 40¢

___ **Miller, Robert M.** 1957 "The Protestant churches and lynching: 1919–1939." Journal of Negro History, pp. 118–131. **BC–205**/67586 40¢

___ **Parsons, Talcott** 1944 "The theoretical development of the sociology of religion: a chapter in the history of modern social science." Journal of the History of Ideas, pp. 176–190 **S–220**/66616 40¢

___ **Pfautz, Harold W.** 1956 "Christian Science: a case study of the social psychological aspect of secularization." Social Forces, pp. 246–251. **S–222**/66618 40¢

___ **Pope, Liston** 1948 "Religion and the class structure." The Annals, pp. 84–91. **S–225**/66621 40¢

___ **Schneider, Louis and Sanford M. Dornbusch** 1957 "Inspirational religious literature: from latent to manifest functions of religion." American Journal of Sociology, pp. 476–481. **S–249**/66640 40¢

___ **Wallace, Anthony F. C.** 1956 "Revitalization movements: some theoretical considerations for their comparative study." American Anthropologist, pp. 264–281. **A–230**/64184 40¢

___ **Warner, R. Stephen** 1970 "The role of religious ideas and the use of models in Max Weber's comparative studies of non-capitalist societies." Journal of Economic History, pp. 74–99. **S–771**/68788 60¢

___ **Wilson, Bryan R.** 1959 "An analysis of sect development." American Sociological Review, pp. 3–15. **S–316**/66695 40¢

The Bobbs-Merrill Company, Inc.
College Division
4300 West 62nd Street
Indianapolis, Indiana 46268

Instructors ordering for class use will receive *upon request* a complimentary desk copy of each title ordered in quantities of 10 or more. Refer to author and *complete* letter-number code when ordering reprints.

☐ Payment enclosed   ☐ Bill me (on orders for $5 or more only)

_____ Course number   _____ Expected enrollment

☐ For examination   ☐ Desk copy

Bill To _____

ADDRESS _____

CITY _____ STATE _____ ZIP _____

Ship To _____

ADDRESS _____

CITY _____ STATE _____ ZIP _____

Please send me _____ copies of the sociology reprints catalog.

Please send me related reprints catalogs in _____

_____

Any reseller is free to charge whatever price he wishes for our books.

For your convenience please use complete form when placing your order.